At the End of the Ferry

Welcome to seasons of joy
In a little bit of Scandinavia
On the Olympic Peninsula

Susan Walters

PRESS

Dedication

S pecial love and thanks to my writing mentor Norm Rohrer who
created the book title. And to Ron Walters whose hard work
and prayers helped make this northwest lifestyle our road less trav-
elled.

"At the End of the Ferry is just absolutely the most delightful read...the kind of thing that you cry for the beauty of it.. Love that. We need that."

Peggy Campbell
President Ambassador Advertising
Chairman of the Board Azusa Pacific University

"Let your boat of life be light." Jerome Klapka Jerome 'This is what Susan Walters ' book is about. It's a way to live and love life.'

Antone B. Pryor, Ph.D.
Psychologist
former adjunct professor University of Colorado
former adjunct professor University of Maryland

We are kindred spirits! Your book is what my soul has been longing for... peace! I love your writing. You make the words pop out of the page. You made my whole day. I was lucky enough to not have to go out and report this morning (doing the noon weather forecast) so I sat and read your book and it was a TRUE treat.

Reading "At the End of the Ferry" was a delightful glimpse into a world most of us only dream of. My mind truly escaped from the busyness and stress of this life. While I read Suzy's words, I got completely lost...lost in the sound of the waves crashing on the seawall and the smell of homemade soup.

It made me want to book a one-way ticket to the peninsula and experience the wonder for myself. But instead I'll just reread "At the End of the Ferry" and get lost again. And again. And again.

Katie Baker
Meteorologist /Reporter
CBS 5 News
Phoenix, Arizona
mother of 3 young children

"I found your words very charming and provocative, not in the sense of disagreement, etc, but in the sense of provoking emotions and enlivening encouragement to be more aware of my surroundings and every experience as a God-gift.. "

"SUSAN BRINGS THE SOUNDS OF SEAGULLS, THE SMELLS OF SALTWATER, THE SIGHTS OF SUNSETS--CLOUDS, AND RAINDROPS, AND THE TASTE OF COOKIES----ALIVE. SHE REMINDS ME, IN RACHAEL CARLSON STYLE, TO CELEBRATE GOD'S EVERYDAY GIFTS.

"EVERYDAY, EVERY SEASON, EVERY OCCASION FOR JOY IS CAPTURED IN LANGUAGE THAT STIRS THE MEMORY AND REMINDS ME TO CELEBRATE THE NORMAL"

"SUSAN SEES THE EXTRAORDINARY IN THE 'ORDINARY'.

Gordon C. Hess,Ph.D.
Adult, Marriage and Family Therapy
Montecito, California

Preface

*I*n these times of unpredictable change, financial uncertainty, and the loss of promise and potential, there is grieving. In these tides of change—the high tides and low tides of life—many of us wonder, "Will it ever be different?" It is the question of our time.

My hope is that as you read about life in a small town of the Pacific Northwest, you will find joy and smile, maybe even forget your worries for a while. I also hope that my story will cause you to focus on God's many wonders and gifts to all of us.

My good fortune is to live on an acre of wooded land at the edge of a bay located across Puget Sound from northern Seattle. Beauty and serenity abound in this sylvan paradise by the sea. The rich world of flora and fauna teems with relics of the Scandinavians who farmed, fished, and logged this area one hundred years ago. The faithful heirs of this haven lovingly tend the gardens and forests that are alive with rich colors. The area is home to eagles, river otters, pheasants, sea lions, and bears. To experience for myself the world that existed a century ago is my privilege to describe. You can improve on some things—you can't improve on this world at all.

My waterfront is a noise, a smell, a feeling. I think the blue heron and gulls know me. Someone called Puget Sound an inland sea. It is our doorway to the Orient and the Pacific Far North. We're close to a big city, yet worlds away from the din of metropolitan living. Nine-thousand-plus neighbors and friends enjoy this secluded, unspoiled spot with my husband Ron and me. Ron travels extensively and needs this retreat for rest and recuperation. After spending twenty years selling real estate I, too, enjoy this pastoral life and would like to share with you a daily diary of life by the bay on the Olympic Peninsula.

Henry David Thoreau beautifully expresses my thoughts about this paradise I live in. He said that he went to the woods "because I wished to live deliberately, to front only the essential facts of life, and see if I could not learn what it had to teach, and not, when I came to die, discover that I had not lived."

North by Northwest

Leave the din of the city and join me on a tour of our treasured peninsula in the northwestern United States. Let's begin by stepping into my kitchen so you can sample the fruit of the land picked from my garden. Notice outside the beautiful weather and wildlife on the move.

Beyond our forest lies metropolitan Seattle, a city first visited by Spanish, American, and British explorers. The state's motto is Al-Ki, meaning "by and by," and reflects the Native American heritage. It is home to such diverse celebrities as the late singer Bing Crosby, the late guitarist Jimi Hendrix, actress Dyan Cannon, Microsoft magnates Bill Gates, Paul Allen and many more. To get to my part of the state, you must cross a steel-reinforced bridge, travel approximately ten miles of open highway, and enjoy one surprisingly reliable thirty-minute ferryboat ride from Seattle.

On many summer nights at our home, we sleep outside under the stars on our deck and are awakened by the sounds of wildlife. The blue heron talks in his sleep in a low, gravelly voice. One night a river otter sampled our beach then gracefully swam away.

We face a saltwater inlet from the Pacific Ocean with ninety feet of shoreline. The sounds of surf and the cry of seagulls are constant background music. Our apple orchard was planted by our neighbor's grandfather in 1910. Today, two generations later, two spinster sisters in their late eighties arrive from Seattle every week to care for, what I call, "A Secret Garden." Our neighbor to the north is another multi-generational family, having been on location for over 100 years.

Just down the road, another family has moved into their grandparents' old farmhouse. They are raising their four children on the old homestead. After all these years, the barn is still intact.

How we found our acre of land is, to us, a miracle. We are the second owners of this land. A long-time resident had become widowed, and all her family lived out of state. As soon as we saw the For Sale sign, we jumped at the opportunity. Our purchase, however, was not without its challenges. There was only one well for water—that was about it. Also, Ron was working out of state, so I became a pioneer woman and faced alone my biggest challenge in real estate. Everything I had learned in the outside world proved to be quite helpful. But then, for this I was born. "You must do the things you think you cannot do," as First Lady Eleanor Roosevelt once said.

Come. Enjoy with me my life beside the sea, among the forests, under azure skies, and above the din of life beyond the end of the ferry line.

> A little house, a house of my own,
> Out of the wind's and rain's way.
> —Padraic Colum

January

Snow flurries are followed by a full moon as this first month of the year begins. January is homemade-soup month at our house, which makes me think of our tureen in the kitchen cupboard, a favorite piece of furniture to our neighbors' children.

Its collection features bright things, most of them red. Let's see, there are red enamel cups and saucers, Aunt Mabel's red teapot that reads "Aunty Mabel's Jam," a little clay pot with red silk geraniums, a red clock, a sign that says "Uff Da," beeswax candles, a jar of red buttons, and a jar of white buttons.

One young neighbor was somewhat worried after spotting the contents of our cupboard. As he left, he said, "Don't forget to put away your Christmas dishes." But they remain a permanent fixture all year round in that wonderful glass cupboard.

The occasion causes me to remember a line from a poem titled "The Cupboard" by Walter de la Mare:

> I know a little cupboard with a teeny tiny key,
> And there's a jar of lollipops for me, me, me.

I guess that magic still captures the curiosity of young and old.

A worker at our property relayed a story of his grandmother's home. In her kitchen one drawer was designated as the lollipop drawer. And as many times as he visited granny, "I would always find a lollipop." Many years later after the house was broken down and abandoned the grandson found his way back to retrieve one cherished treasure—the lollipop drawer. With that historical backdrop we created a lollipop drawer in our own kitchen.

January is, for me, a time to rest and be reenergized.

January 1

A few crocuses are up. I made granola chocolate-chip cookies today. Three pheasants visited our yard. We watched the Rose Bowl game.

January 5

Today I cooked halibut. Big, wet snowflakes cover the ground. I took down the Christmas decorations.

January 7

A stop at the hardware store proved to be productive. Back home, I brought branches of red dogwood inside to force their bloom. I couldn't help but notice a peanut shell buried in a seashell near the dogwood bush.

January 12

I read again Rick Bass's *Winter*. Thunderclouds signal a cold front from Canada.

January 14

A blue hue painted the water at 7:30 a.m. Later moonlight dazzled the bay, and the smelt shimmered in the light. The rippling water was hypnotizing.

January 16

The cold has silenced the chipmunks, squirrels, and birds. I guess they're sleeping in. Even mice need to keep warm. One ran out from under a pile of rocks and seashells. I remember that Robert Burns wrote in *To a Mouse*, "Wee, sleek-it, cowering, timorous beastie."

The heavy snow storm last night left us without power and made driving difficult. Rich and Wendy called and asked if I needed anything; this made me feel good.

Whose footprints are these in the snow? It looks like the prints of a fisher—a recently endangered species of the weasel family.

January 19
There was sunshine today. I watched the movie *The Quiet Man*, starring John Wayne and Maureen O'Hara. There was a fine snow in the night, but most of it melted the next day.

January 23
I discovered icicles on the old shed. The snow is staying; the temperature is thirty degrees. I made cauliflower soup and onion-dill bread.

Great Gale of Wind
"Had a big wind storm here yesterday," said the Kansas farmer,
"that blew away my house, my wife, and my three children."
"That's terrible! But why aren't you looking for them?"
"No use. Wind'll change next week and they'll come back."
—B. A. Botkin
Folklore compiler

January 27
It was about fifteen degrees today. I wrote and watched from the window as waves crashed over our seawall.

January 30
Today is another beautiful day of sunshine. Some writings by John Baillie from *The Diary of Private Prayer* seem appropriate.

Lord, Maker of all things, I praise Thee for the
light that now streams through my windows.
I praise Thee for the sea, for scudding cloud and
singing bird.
I praise Thee for music and books and
good company.
As the light of day streams through these
Windows and floods this room, so let me open the windows
of my heart.
Forbid that I should walk through Thy beautiful
world with unseeing eyes.

February

*I*n our bay, we don't have many shipwrecks, certainly not the number that Seattle does. That Space-Needled city has an unusual way of greeting some of its seagoing visitors. For example, a fully rigged sailing ship sank decades ago with its rich cargo of canned Alaskan salmon. The vessel may still be there, preserved in the cold brine.

Of course, that's nothing compared to the story I read of the Japanese ghost ship that "drifted aimlessly for five thousand miles with mummified fishermen aboard. An agony-filled diary was found onboard to fill in history's blanks."

But Seattle does boast a pair of sunken restaurant ships. For whatever reason, they both just capsized. It gives a whole new meaning to the word *tip*.

Yes, the waterways of Puget Sound are full of adventure.

"The seas and everything that moves" in the sea praises Him (Psalm 69:34). (NASB)

February 1

The two men who abandoned their small fishing boat today just two hundred yards in front of our bulkhead won't be the subjects of any blockbuster movies. They didn't have to brave the cold or drift aimlessly for days. Nor did they have to survive by eating barnacles or raw turtle meat. Though rescued by the Coast Guard, they did provide lessons to be learned by anyone who might go down to the sea someday.

When the wind comes down the seventeen-mile channel, it uses our home as its bull's-eye. There is no doubt when it arrives. On those jaw-clenching days, it's a good thing to have any outdoor chores already done.

Even though this is a bay, the water can get rough at times. As I looked out the window, I saw the small fishing boat in trouble. The boat was sinking. I'd never seen anything like this. Neighbors were gathering on their beaches. Help had been called, but darkness made rescue dangerous.

At first, I didn't see the fishermen, but then I saw two men in a tiny dinghy with no oars. Where was the help? It was too dangerous to take a boat out there ourselves to try to rescue the sailors.

Obviously, fear gripped the hearts of the two men. Their fishing vessel sank lower and lower in the water. Finally the Coast Guard appeared. The two men were pulled aboard to safety. Later I discovered their boat drifted to shore.

February 2

This morning the fishing boat was towed away. I walked the beach at low tide so I could gather information to tell the story to my eight-year-old niece, Jaclyn. All along our beach, items from the boat were floating ashore.

I put together a shipwreck box for Jaclyn. It contained a little jar of instant coffee with a red lid, a plastic tray that was also bright red, and a baseball. Sand stuck to everything. She is going to find treasures from the bottom of the sea in her shipwreck box. Other things came ashore later: an oar, a map, and an old kerosene lantern.

February 4

Ron has the day off after traveling to Tampa and Minneapolis, so he puttered in his workshop. I wrote most of the day. Big wet snowflakes are falling.

February 5

The smelt run from mid-September through February. Smelt can grow to nine inches in length and in the moonlight give off a shimmer from the natural silver band along their side. They tend to gather in the pockets of eelgrass that grow in the sandy soil along the median high tide.

A neighbor man knocked at my back door with a "can't miss" proposition: he wanted to catch smelt off my beach, and in return he'd give me half the haul, cleaned and ready for the frying pan. I smiled and agreed. An hour later, he returned to the same back door with a basket full of the tasty catch—and that was just my half!

Once cleaned, smelt are best prepared with a cornmeal crust and then cooked in oil, cooked just like the way we do trout when camping. Oh my, it was tasty! There was so much left over that I took some to Murry and Nancy. I'm grateful for Murry and the many times he comes to our rescue, such as delivering a generator in a power outage.

As I write, the sky is various colors of blue. Sunshine abounds. I hung a goose down comforter on the clothesline.

February 7

We went to Seattle on the 8:50 a.m. ferry, and I shopped for flannel pajamas. Ron bought a down jacket. We had lunch at 13 Coins.

We bought smoked salmon from the fish market and stocked up on bulk food: yeast, cinnamon, nutmeg, dried onion, dill seed, dried lemon peel, sunflower seeds, and cracked wheat bulgur.

When we got back home, I went outside to brew a pot of honey tea. I sat on the bench stairs in my pajamas and robe.

> May the beauty of winter's rest
> Adorn your hearts with joy
> And you be blessed.
> —Virginia Page Rohrer

I love snow. It falls here only a couple of weeks each winter, if we're lucky. Living at sea level, we consider it a treat when it arrives.

February 13

It's wild and stormy today. I ate blueberry pancakes for lunch.

There is a lot of tree-trunk traffic again. Squirrels chase each other, and a raccoon limps as it forages on our property.

The wind howled all night. Christina Rossetti said in a Christmas carol, "In the bleak midwinter, frosty wind made moan." And last night the wind was moaning.

February 17
Yellow and white forsythia branches are blooming in the house. Tomorrow morning we're meeting Dennis and Gayle for breakfast on the fjord.

I bought jerky and apple sausage at the country meat market. I made Aunt Mabel's blackberry cobbler from frozen berries from the summer. I finished sewing a bun-warmer cover.

February 21
Scott, our neighbor, went fishing. His boat overturned, and he spent the afternoon in our living room, wrapped in a blanket. His house keys went down with the tackle box. He is only one casualty among many this month who have suffered boating incidents. Fortunate outcomes, all, thankfully.

February 25
I enjoyed soup for supper with brown bread. I put out suet for the birds.

Walking home from town after lunch with a friend, I noticed a new family in one of the older homes in the neighborhood: an osprey had been moved out by a female bald eagle that needed more room for her eaglets.

February 27
Another snowstorm today.

Snow
The fence posts wear marshmallow hats
On a snowy day.
Bushes in their nightgowns
Are kneeling down to pray
—Dorothy Aldis

One of my favorite children's stories is "The Snowman":

> So the north wind came along and blew him
> out the door. Now there's nothing left of him
> but a puddle on the floor.
> —Author Unknown

Snow makes me feel like the world is disappearing. It's serene and quiet. There's not much traffic on our road. "The best part of living in the country," thought Evan Esar "is the people you don't meet." So today we stay home and cocoon.

I walked to our country store across the street. Donald and Kathy had the wood-stove pumping out warmth. I didn't want to leave. Winter brings to me the beauty of uninterrupted thought, the calm of hibernating with books and pots of tea on a Sunday afternoon.

Ron and I had a baby eagle fly through our workshop window. The eaglet was okay and flew back out, but shattered glass lay everywhere. Our neighbor Murry and Ron put new glass back into the window. The few feathers the eaglet lost were beautiful.

Wildlife has been aggressive this month. I wonder what that means. I fed the birds throughout the winter with a new mixture of seeds, and four kinds of woodpeckers have taken turns trying the recipe.

I am thankful to the Lord for this day's happiness. My heart is filled with gratitude for all the sights and sounds around me. . . for the peace of the country and the pleasant bustle of the town. . . for friends. . . for work. . . for play when the day's work is done.

Close by the jolly fire
I sit to warm my frozen bones a bit
The cold wind burns my face and blows
Its frosty pepper up my nose.
And tree, house and hill and lake are frosted
Like a wedding cake.
— Robert Frost

March

I've met only two people who have ever eaten a blue heron. It was an older couple, clients of mine when I was in the business world. They sat in my office one day telling of the hard times in their young married years. One Christmas they had an apple tree, so they could do plenty of things with apples. But there was no money for a turkey. They shot, dressed, and stuffed a blue heron for Christmas dinner. "It didn't taste bad" was the assessment of the diners.

My favorite things by far are wildlife: the blue heron that talks in its sleep, the call of the loon, smelt and herring with their iridescent shimmer when the moon is out, swallows, starlings, chickadees, pheasants, crows, ducks and gulls.

My least favorite topic is death, but it steals into all our lives. I left out a bucket of water in which three baby chipmunks drowned. Another time, within a few weeks of each other, two young raccoons died. One injured itself on our beach stairs. The other knocked the birdbath over on himself.

There are blossoming pear trees: Bosc and Comice. They are house warming gifts from Katherine and Jeff who live in San Francisco.

The woods are carpeted with primroses.

I look forward to the time when I can collect the empress trees' seedpods. I remember reading that many years ago in China, enterprising merchants used chestnut seedpods as shipping material, much like we use Styrofoam or wadded-up newspaper. I've often wished, had I lived in those days, that I could have received a package from Singapore or Shanghai filled with flavorful teas and spices. No doubt I'd have found a favorite jar for storing the tea and spices, but the packer's seedpods might have been an even greater treasure.

Carpets of thyme are spreading, and wooly gray lamb's ears are blooming. I admit my weakness in the garden. I can't pass lamb's ears without stopping to rub its fuzzy soft leaf between my thumb and forefinger. It's an addiction I have no intention of addressing.

Out along the driveway, both pink dogwoods are ablaze—that is, if you can call a subtle, dusk-like hue a "blaze." Blossoms are popping out of the cherry trees and out of the Bosc and Comice pear trees too.

March 1

I dug in the garden today. I lost all my dahlias; the winter was just too cold, despite all the mulch I piled on them. I discovered a landscape find while digging. It was an old dog tag with the name *Danny* inscribed on it.

March 2

Popovers and homemade chili for supper.

During the past year, Ron has flown to Oakland, San Francisco, San Jose, San Diego, L.A., Denver, Colorado Springs, Dallas, Phoenix, San Antonio, Portland, and Bozeman. Life is full.

I wrote fifty-eight pages of my book in two days. The office where I'm working right now is an outbuilding of sorts. It has no foundation and is of Lilliputian dimension—extremely small. But it's sufficient and quiet. It also has a heated floor.

Trillium blossoms opening in March are another of my favorite things. The dahlias, given to me by my friend Lauren, finally found their way into the spring soil. The occasion called for more flowers, so in went my 'Country Girl' geranium that has been wintering in the potting shed. I've always loved 'Country Girl'. When I first saw her name tag at the farmers' market some years ago, I couldn't pass it up—it cost a whole dollar!

March 5

We had a surprise March snow—it was beautiful. Ron and I played in it at night.

I took a picture of Ron as he shuttled home from California with briefcase in hand. The next morning on the waterfront, while still in our pajamas, we drank steaming coffee and took in the stunning but oh-so-cold beauty.

Up here, winter is a time for rejuvenation. The snow is so quiet and fresh that it energizes me.

We had chili and Grandma Pipho's Johnnycake for supper. Johnnycake is a cornmeal flatbread that was an early American food.

March 6

There's a warm wind today. The first pale-yellow primroses are in bloom. Mom and dad hawks trade off feeding their baby hawks. One parent dropped a snake in the big nest.

March 7

Beads of rain formed on my window this morning. I helped Ron and Erin plant shrubs. My late movie treat was *Meet Me in St. Louis*.

March 11

Early morning wind chill is twenty-eight degrees. The geese arrived just ahead of the thunder snow.

March 15

I wrote from 3:00 a.m. until noon.

March 18

This morning's efforts netted six pounds of freshly caught King Salmon in the freezer, and a freshly made loaf of gingerbread I baked this morning sits on the table. Meanwhile the hummingbirds are waiting for their feeders.

Palm Sunday

Church was especially meaningful this morning. The service began with the youth waving palm branches in unison as they walked down the middle aisle. The meaning of the event wasn't lost on Ron or me.

March 22

An old weathered wooden WELCOME sign washed up on our beach, so we nailed it onto our gate. Our one-hundred-foot-deep artesian well was serviced. An oyster boat worked in front of our place. I sewed a flannel nightgown for Aunt Lucille.

Dennis, Joan, Ron, and I upholstered our kitchen chairs with black-and-white checkered fabric.

March 24

I took an Easter basket to our neighbor and saw Jeff's boat heading for town. I cooked beets and used the colored water for dying Easter eggs. In high school my sisters and I would slice off a portion of an uncooked beet to use as rouge on our cheeks.

Easter Sunday

Ron and I went to church. Trillium blossoms are blooming. 'Pink Diamond' tulips are bursting open on our porch. I took a picture of them and delivered Easter cards to our friends. Tulips are mesmerizing. Rain falls while the sun shines.

At the Easter tea party for the neighbor children, the girls wore their Easter dresses, and we spent time in the garden. I think of the words of Peggy Crapple:

> Don't plan to double dig the perennial
> Border the same afternoon
> You're having a garden club!

The hot-pink hyacinths are the attention-getters this year.

I'm reminded of planning and planting this garden. To me, personal pleasure awaits the willing amateurs who begin a garden from scratch and keep at it until they create their beautiful, flower-filled oases.

My seven garden rooms sprout personalities of their own. The garden to the northwest of the well continues a tradition dating back for decades. It seems that in every home we've lived irises have been there too. These particular rhizomes have been planted, dug up, and replanted during multiple job transfers and have inhabited the soils of three states. This is my humble private garden. This is my heart's ease.

> Garden's where the
> Soul's at ease.
> —W. B. Yeats

I still find scraps of paper from the dry cleaners or restaurant napkins where I jotted down ideas: "Find a natural birdbath rock. . . build a picnic table path. . . put sprinklers in the planter. . . install an outdoor shower. . . build a picket fence. . . get dirt off the white picket fence. . . build an arbor near the house entrance with the same pitch to the roof as the house. . . find a supplier for Australian grass. . . get Murry to identify power lines. . . plant the Shasta daisy seeds that Dan gave you. . . put in plants for hummingbirds. . . plant butterfly bushes. . . bury five hundred daffodil bulbs. . . move laurel to create a hedge. . . move the cherry tree and buy a gull birdbath."

Oh, where did I plant the comfrey?

> But though an old man, I am but a young gardener.
> —Thomas Jefferson in a letter to Charles Wilson Peals
> August 20, 1811

March 27

We say, "Fog on the fjord" when there's fog over the bay. It's a sure sign that the weather is changing. Soon there will be a symphony of foghorns on the bay: toots, honks, and low-sounding booms.

I piled wood, worked in the woods, and watched *Murphy's Romance*.

> March brings breezes loud and shrill,
> Stirs the dancing daffodil.
> —Sara Coleridge

March 28

Scott and Patty stopped by. Ron spent the afternoon reading in our home library. A hailstorm hit.

March 29

Sandpipers and plovers are on the beach. The chipmunk on the fence is chattering about something.

April

*T*here's a saying in our area, "If you *can't* see Mount Rainier, it's raining. If you *can* see Mount Rainier, it's about to rain." There's a beautiful view of Mount Rainier today. It rained!

I found a robin's nest amongst the Oregon grape and holly bushes. There they were—four undisturbed grayish, spotted eggs. The mother, who had apparently darted off for a quick meal of wild elderberries, was voicing her displeasure that I was nearby. Or maybe she was apologizing for breaking the cardinal rule of mother birds being absent during the hatching of their eggs.

Euphorbia, a wood spurge, is popping up everywhere.

Our favorite plant is the 'Royal Purple' smoke tree. Its bronzy smoke puffs with purple-red foliage have a tendency to grow out as much as up.

Wooly thyme, a soft purple ground cover with carpet-like color and cushion, serves to soften the broken chunks of concrete and aggregate steps. If you could somehow graft your nose onto your shoe, you'd be able to smell the lavender aroma as you walk upon its wooly carpet. On more than one occasion, I've wondered if I could rip out my living room rug and replace it with a carpet of wooly thyme.

Vita Sackville West says, "Gardening is like matchmaking, full of marriages and divorces."

April Fool's Day
You can see Mount Rainier. I started to sneeze after just *hearing* the lawn mower.

April 3
It's colder today and raining. The sound of spring's rain is mesmerizing. My favorite rains are those that come when the sun is shining too. The pink and white heather and heath are aglow. 'Chocolate Chip' ajuga is showing its stuff. It has spikes of blue flowers above small chocolate-covered leaves.

April 4
The weather is sultry. I made cabbage soup. Dan brought us some fresh crab.

It was another beautiful day. I worked out in the woods. Erin and I trimmed the giant ferns.

April 6
The pink camellias are blooming. I made a fire in the fire pit. Cowslips are blooming along the road. I saw my first salamander. I was intrigued when I found a frog sleeping under a rock. Ferns are unfurling their leaves.

April 7
I met Debbie at the tearoom downtown. It was a cloudy, cold, and windy day. I played Christmas tapes all day. There's nothing like Christmas music to lift your spirits. . . even in April. The birch trees outside were swaying to the music.

April 8
I got eggs from the island today. We've never known the egg rancher's name, but only refer to him as the "egg man." His ranch is up a long, winding driveway past two ponds flooded with geese, ducks, and visiting migratory foul. Every egg run is met with new wonders on that pond. The self-service outbuilding, where the eggs are kept in an old but reliable refrigerator, is located just across from the classic brick farmhouse.

The egg man must have been sleeping in this morning because as I was putting the eggs in the car, he raised an upstairs dormer window, leaned out in his plaid pajamas, and hollered, "Are there enough eggs down there?" I waved my approval and apologized for waking him. He just smiled, laughed, and, presumably went back to bed. Only then did I realize I'd been writing through the night and it was before 6:00 a.m.

April 9
Quite a few tree limbs blew down in the night. I found the lifeless body of a large baby bird that must have fallen out of its nest.

April 10
Ron and I were invited to a salmon dinner with friends. Our contribution was homemade onion-dill bread.

April 11
Brea and Logan helped us plant fifteen baby trees in our yard: snake bark maple, 'Bloodgood' maple, 'King' apple, and two chestnuts that Logan grew from seed.

April 15
There was a brief hailstorm while Patty, Benjamin, and I were at the park. We laughed hysterically as we tried to find cover from the hail. Ben found a big banana slug under a rock. We screamed at the seven inch critter.

April 16
Today was the opening day of fishing; the weather was cold. I had fresh halibut for lunch.

April 17
I met Scott and Margaret for dinner at the Coleman dock in Seattle. We stood in a long line at Ivar's walk-a-way fish and chip stand.

April 21
It's Earth Day. Ron and I went to Vashon Island to pick up another snake bark maple tree and a red paperbark maple. Planting trees and gardening are forms of therapy for me, be it Earth Day or any other day. Today was aerobic gardening, and I'm sure I'll be sore tomorrow.

I read with intrigue an article titled "Softly by the Sea." Our bay is anything but soft. This winter's waves were wild and made me fear I'd lose my plantings. I'm told lavender and rosemary are hearty enough to withstand waves and salt spray. Crocosmia, hydrangea, sedum, and hostas also stand up to the storms of the Northwest.

I fertilized the lawn on this cloudy day. We built a fire on the beach and roasted Margaret's homemade marshmallows. Forty Siberian snow geese camped in front of our home. We heard the geese talking all night.

Fragaria 'Lipstick' (alpine strawberry) ground cover is sprouting up everywhere. It has hot-pink flowers galore. I forgot I had planted *Cimicifuga* 'Brunette'; it was popping out of the ground. Its dark-purple foliage with pink spike flowers is fragrant in the summer.

April 25

Ron drained our thousand-gallon water tank in the pump house. Our twelve-year-old godson kayaked to our house for the first time. What a surprise to see this eager spirit land on our beach!

April 26

We lost power twice. High tides brought in an old rowboat.

We stopped by our used bookstore in town. Ron had packed the trunk of the car with literary treasures we'd read long ago. The books needed a new home. We were compensated with $330 as payment for the mini library. While there I bought gardening books and Ron bought a set of encyclopedias.

I made bean soup and turkey stock. I also made a popcorn mold in the shape of a lamb.

April 29

Five hundred daffodil bulbs are in bloom along our driveway. A mother seal was resting on the float this morning while we ate breakfast. Her crying baby was clinging to a nearby buoy.

Roz rode her bike to my house, and I gave her a tour of my gardens. While here she couldn't help but notice my pheasant's eye bulbs in full bloom. The quince is ablaze.

May

*M*ay Day is a favorite Russian holiday. It has something to do with the labor unions and the tyranny they experienced under years of dictatorship.

Over the years, Russian peasants have used flowers to celebrate the day. It came as a surprise to me when one May Day I found a basket of flowers hanging on our front door. We're not Russian. We don't even know any Russians. Other than having the ability to whip up a mean stroganoff, we don't know much about Russian culture. But it wasn't long before Ralph West, an old friend of ours, called to identify the gesture of flowers. We hadn't seen Ralph and his wife, Beth, for some time, so it was a warm reminder of a good friendship. I wonder if Ralph is Russian. . .

Ron and I took a weekend trip—a holiday, as our Canadian hosts call it—to Victoria, British Columbia. We traveled aboard the Black Ball Ferry out of Port Angeles. It's a great hour and a half ride. We passed a pod of orca whales as they made their annual migratory trip to cooler waters up north. On the way, they hung a right at the Straits of Juan de Fuca for a rich salmon lunch. From the size of those mammals, I'd say they had a long, long lunch.

> Earth herself is adorning, this sweet May morning.
> —William Wordsworth in "Ode"

Twice a day the tides roll into our deep saltwater bay. Science says they're drawn by the moon, but I suspect they have a pact with the hungry gulls. The swelling of the waters brings crabs and shrimp and every delicacy known to birds. Kingfishers, great blue herons, eagles—they all feast from nature's show-and-tell. Yes, the birds know the tides well. And so do we.

In our neck of the woods, there are two schedules that every person lives by: the ferry schedule and the tide schedule. Therefore, every January Ron and I post these two timetables in our mud porch.

The tide seems to have an effect on us all. Shakespeare in *Julius Caesar* wrote, "There is a tide in the affairs of men." And so there is. It would appear that God sovereignly puts tides within us all. Certainly Job experienced intense high and low tides through the storms he weathered.

Three families of chickadees raised their chicks in one birdhouse this spring.

Ours is a rock beach. It requires a good pair of soles to explore its bounty. To the east is an alluring sandbar that begs you to walk its way. And so I did. But no one told me about the quicksand holes. They're not dangerous. You can't be swallowed up in them, but I've lost more than one boot to those sneaky thieves.

To the west, the sea grows eelgrass and algae, a favorite of the migratory snow geese. When the tide subsides just before daybreak, the geese treat the grasses as their personal smorgasbord. Their noisy glee is a wake-up call for everyone. My husband and I love the morning bellows, but the great blue heron that sleeps high atop a nearby fir tree is not a bit happy. His low, gravelly response voices his displeasure. But that doesn't quiet the gaggle of gorging geese.

The tide brings other treasures also: beautiful driftwood and shipwrecked items. But most of all, it brings a sense of newness, a fresh start. Poet John Masefield knew the tide: "I must go down to the seas again, for the call of the running tide is a wild call and a clear call that may not be denied."

May 4

I visited the island woods this evening.

There's a strong vine of sweet peas lining the bulkhead, though we call them "beach peas." They're a hearty strain and can do what few other seashore plants can: the closer they get to the salt air and crashing waves, the more they thrive. And whereas they must have a breaking point somewhere—after all, even crabs have to walk away from the sea sometimes—the beach peas seem to love their seaside home.

On the opposite side of the yard stands the stately iris, who wants nothing to do with the beach, the gulls, and certainly not that gang of sea-loving beach peas.

Did I mention I love tulips? Another layer is in bloom. I'm not sure I could survive a spring without tulips. They're my right of passage.

And so are the peonies. The 'Karl Rosenfeld' is my favorite of the peonies, and it, too, is about to burst open. Why do these little teases make me wait? I'm not sure why I'm so partial to them. Perhaps it's because they're one of God's showiest flowers. Their audacious red blooms are four inches wide and showcase brilliantly against their dark-green foliage. And to say they're hearty is demeaning. I have it on very good authority that my peonies will live another fifty years. The resilient 'Karl Rosenfeld' will probably attend my funeral, but I won't be at his.

May is a month of tides and so much more: A female duck is nesting on our property. Also, I found a squirrel's nest in a tree trunk. Lots of tree-trunk traffic is taking place. I discovered a hummingbird nest near the workshop.

The town matriarch, Elsie, died at the age of 101. At sunset the church bells rang some of Elsie's favorite hymns.

May 5

The weather is unpredictable. I brought in the potted geraniums.

We're wearing wool coats and thermals as we enjoy coffee in the garden.

I'm making a whole-wheat, cinnamon-pecan coffee cake. It turned into a cook-off, producing enough baked goods for the next week.

I transplanted Tillie, the nickname for our trillium, to a shadier location.

'Mrs. Furnival', our favorite rhododendron, is in full bloom. She has light-pink flowers with a splashy red blotch on large trusses.

May 10

A flotilla of pleasure crafts have moored in the bay. The six of them had a barbecue, and two more boats joined them overnight. The conduit-like surface of saltwater made their voices sound like they were in my kitchen. They wanted to know if the coffee was ready. It was.

That evening a seaplane used our bay for a series of touch-and-go landings.

We had another brief hailstorm.

Scott and Patty brought us some mussels from their underwater farm. Soon the delicacies were in a skillet, up to their necks in white wine. We had too many mussels, so Jim and Lorraine were the lucky recipients of the extras.

May 12

The baby geese are being taught the art of survival by two no-nonsense parents.

I took a long walk to the marina. I don't think I've ever seen that shade of orange in a sunset before.

Springtime is anything but tidy. We had some lightning today and even a funnel cloud. Watch the tide and you'll know when the fish are biting.

May 14

A local handyman stopped by to give me a bid on a picket fence. But before I could greet him, he had returned to his truck to leave because he had seen our decorative Gone Fishing sign by the front door and decided we were busy with more important work. I hollered to him just in time.

I found a colorful baby-bird feather on our covered porch. Another find was a frog croaking in a pot by the front door.

The quince is showing its radiant orange color. I'd better be careful; the stinging nettle appears ready for battle. But the real surprise was the blaze of the 'Pink Diamond' tulips outside the window.

Up and down the road blossom a new batch of buttercups.

The birds sing so loudly they drown out the croaking frogs.

First Day of spring

> Birds that cannot even sing
> Dare to come again in spring!
> —Edna St. Vincent Millay

May 18

The bog today was full of yellow irises. Awaiting me in the potting shed were several chores—sorting through my flower seeds, sharpening my pruning shears, and listing items I need from the nursery.

May 22

I found four dead snakes in the bird bath this week. The crows or the eagles are dropping them in the water to wash them. My guess is to feed their babies.

May 28

The chickadee makes a trail through the clover looking for bugs. Today I mixed lavender, rosemary and cinnamon sticks—I saw this on television. I crushed them altogether and tied them in a sock. The relaxing fragrance is a perfect de-compressor at the end of the day.

June

*O*n our back porch is an old breadbox that serves as a local mailbox. It's not for the postal carrier; he doesn't even know it's there. Truth be told, we're not even sure ourselves how long it's been there. But it's not so much a box of mystery as it is a drop-off box for our neighbors.

Ten-year-old Logan rode his bike up the driveway with a note from his mom and a canister of blueberries. It didn't even occur to Logan that he might ring the bell or knock. He knows where the box is; he's spent many of his growing-up days serving as a courier between his house and that box. And sure enough, as I walked out the door, all I could see was the trail of his bike and some fallen berries spilled on the driveway.

This morning sandpipers congregated at the sea edge. Witter Bynner describes these vigilant critters as follows: "Now he stiffens, now he wilts, like a little boy on stilts."

There's a full moon over the tall firs in the forest. Soon it will move over the bay. When it shines on us as we sleep, we call it "moon bathing."

This is my first summer off from business in seventeen years. The first thing I wanted to do was go barefoot in my yard all day. It didn't take long to feel at home.

My greeters were many: butterflies dancing from bush to bush, birds following my lead as we dodged the sprinkler twisting round and round, dragonflies flitting here and there, and even a garden snake peeking through the slats of a picket fence, wondering who the shoeless human was.

My survey of the beach turned up raccoon footprints. From the way they two-stepped, I imagine the furry beast met with a sizable crab that wasn't willing to go easily. Just then an eagle swooped down to snag a surprised salmon. Dinner was served in the nearest tall fir.

It's not uncommon for logs to beach themselves on our property, but one day a picnic table did the same. From its weathered condition, it was clear it had been adrift for some time. Dan helped me drag it up over the bulkhead. After scraping off much of its barnacles and sand, Dan re-commissioned it for the summer. We've already had several tea parties and picnics on that table. In fact, my eight-year-old niece, Jaclyn, let out a loud laugh when she saw the dried seaweed still stuck to its underside.

As if turnabout were fair play, a baby bird , who had been trapped indoors all day, flew out the front door when I went into the house this evening after spending a full day in the yard.

June 2

Today a little red rowboat with the name *Rachel* on it glided by. Four or five kids aboard were blowing bubbles from a jar. Then a kayak passed, and we all waved to each other.

June 3

The air is still. I was awakened from my nap by hail. The pink wild rose is blooming all through the hedgerows and thickets. I saw a grass snake. A pair of mallards are sunning on our lawn.

Several June days have already been in the eighties. A snake was keeping cool around the rose bush I watered this morning. Thankfully, Washington State is well known for having no poisonous snakes, at least, not western Washington.

We've had a heat wave for a week. The clothesline is getting lots of use. The big sunflower comforter is airing, and the goose downs are waving in the breeze.

June is such a celebration of nature. The blue heron sat in the shade of our lone tree on the beach. When he heard me walk by on the gravel, he flew away. It seems as though I stirred lots of wildlife from their cool spots.

Berry blossoms are here en masse. I see a bright-yellow bird with eyelashes and translucent orange beak. Could it be a miniature parakeet?

Bees and hummingbirds like my new garden planted under the magnolia tree.

I lost count, but I must have twenty of 'Mrs. Boxby's' foxgloves; an abundance of chocolate ajuga, Canterbury bells, and 'Autumn Joy' sedum; and hundreds of bulbs. I also have mullein; evening primrose; astilbe; Oriental poppy; hollyhocks; a miniature rose named 'Suzy Q'; pansies; Ron's favorite, sweet William; and nasturtium. Oh, how I love the smell of fresh mulch. Mmmmm!

It was a task, but I planted thirty-nine new trees before the heat wave hit: alpine, blue spruce, cedar, and Douglas fir. We lost our lone White Pine in a storm last winter. Thankfully I've salvaged a few of its pine cones as reminders.

The ever-changing moon on the bay, the blue hue of the water, and the sparkling ripples and sunrises that change the water's colors create an almost tropical setting.

Cindy brought us a salmon from Alaska.

We had another minus (low) tide. Starfish, jellyfish, and moon snails appeared on our beach, not to mention sandpipers, eagles, kingfishers, and three baby otters.

Joan's cat, named Come Come, hadn't been home all week. So I was asked to put food out while Joan visited her brother out of town. Then today Joan opened the pump house door, and guess who was sleeping there? Yes, Come Come!

June 8
A neighbor brought me iris, red *Crocosmia*, and a snowball plant for my garden. I wrote all day under the magnolia tree.

June 10
Oh my, what a beautiful day! Ron and I had bread pudding and tea in town.

Frogs croak in the night. It is a sound we learn to live without
in the city, but it can instantly summon a flood of memories of a
country childhood.
—The National Geographic Society

Walking through the island park, I noticed the wild yellow iris
standing proudly in a foot of water in the pond. Dragonflies were
busy. Nature is like a balm.

Today was a day for my favorite outdoor recipe: manure tea. It's
a favorite pick-me-up for my gardens. The recipe is simple. You take
one large designated twenty-gallon metal washtub, throw in one
scoop of manure, add water, and let it steep for several hours. The
finished product is spread liberally via a sprinkling can. The flowers
just eat it up. The smell is, however, less than desirable—putrid, to
be honest—but the results are magical.

The double yellow angel trumpet is magnificent. But the eye-
pleasing plant serves as nature's good news–bad news conundrum:
the entire plant is quite poisonous.

June 17
Today began with the season's first strawberries, which was the
perfect match for the very warm day. Even the kids are seeking relief
from the heat by spending the day swimming. Jaclyn and some other
kids, as well as the neighbor's dog, spent all day on a raft anchored
out about fifty feet. Some waves gave them quite a ride. She also
went kayaking.

Jaclyn smelled like a fish when she came in. When I took her
and the other kids for ice cream, I said, "Jaclyn, you smell like
fish." Undaunted, she replied, "Aunt Suzy, your sign says, 'Gone
Fishing.'"

June 20
I wish I could describe the smell of spring; certainly it would
include the words *sweet* and *inviting*. When we rode the ferry today,
as we approached the land, we could smell spring.

Heavy early-morning dew blanketed the ground today. The eagles and the otters took turns on the float all day. The humming-bird's eggs have hatched. It was a hot one—up to 90 degrees.

Rain, rain go away. We had Father's Day dinner with my brother, Scotty.

June 21

Today was our wedding anniversary, and we had a late breakfast consisting of Irish bacon and blueberry pancakes.

June 30

It's partly cloudy here and Ron will soon find out about the weather in San Francisco, which is famous for its weather-caused flight delays. Our temperatures are amazingly similar to the Bay Area.

Today I bought a ten-pound bag of sugar to provide nourishment for our hummingbirds. There's a pack of them swarming their favorite feeder. They're going to eat us out of house and home!

I cut several sprigs of rosemary and put them in vases around the house.

Down the beach the sandpipers are parading. Their long legs are busy. They are in a feeding frenzy. Later I saw them rest behind the drift wood with one eye open watching me write. I wonder if they know I'm writing about them.

> The Sandpiper
> Across the narrow beach we flit,
> One little sandpiper and I;
> And fast I gather, bit by bit,
> The scattered driftwood, bleached and dry.
> — Celia Laighton Thaxter

I was reminiscing with a childhood friend, and we were discussing the bounty we now enjoy. But as children, food was rationed in our homes. I remember sitting outside on the porch, shucking peas and eating more than I saved. My siblings and I each got half a cup of orange juice at breakfast. We split a cantaloupe seven ways.

For Sunday breakfasts, we each enjoyed two half slices of bacon (each about two inches long). Sunday dinners, we were allowed one pork chop each. Soda was portioned out at half a glass, but we could have all the popcorn we could eat.

While growing up, we were never financially able to share cookies and homemade rolls with our neighbors. I always wished we could have done more.

> You shall eat the fruit of the labor of your hands;
> you shall be happy, and it shall be well with you.
> —Psalm 128:2

Look what I found: another baby squid in the rain gutter! I wonder what bird dropped him there. Whoever it was, I'm sure he's retracing his flight and looking for the squiggly morsel.

The bay is filled with a myriad of boats and small ships. The boating season is in full throttle.

The hot-pink lupines are busting their buttons—the little show-offs! But it's only fair that they get their turn because soon it will be the primroses that will catch my full attention.

At this time of year, the evenings are long and beautiful. I could sit on my porch for hours admiring the brilliant colors of the chestnut tree. Well, if I'm going to spend hours out here, I'd better reclaim the daybed from the garage.

July

*J*uly greeted me, not with a bang, but with a growl. I disturbed a great blue heron as he was napping and found myself royally chastised by His Greatness.

Barb has a great blue heron named Icky, named in honor of Ichabod Crane.

Let nature be your teacher.
—William Wordsworth

Outdoor picnics are a staple on the table that washed up on our beach. We enjoy fireworks from a barge, and also, red *Crocosmia* are blooming (they, too, look like fireworks). Where do I stop?

In all God's wisdom He created the fly,
and then forgot to tell us why.
—Ogden Nash

July is the month for farmers' markets and Fourth of July ice cream cakes made in the likeness of an American flag. It's watermelons and swimming holes, boats and water skiers, and friends enjoying it all with us on the deck.

Most special to me is reading for hours at a time on the outdoor daybed located next to my south-facing porch with glass on three sides and a sign that reads "Potting Shed." The outdoor daybed provides therapy you can't buy from any therapist.

Cloud Magic
Beneath the comfortable sky
all afternoon I lie
and think about the books I've read.
—Carolyn Davis

I rest, I wander, I reenergize my spirit. I see pictures in the clouds. Oh, July, stay long!

On rainy days, I go to my potting-shed porch and deadhead old red geraniums and prune daisies. It's as much a mud porch as a potting shed, but my preference for the room tends to dignify the place. I have an old watering-can fountain sitting on the black-and-white checkered floor. I write letters here and entertain summer suppers on an English gate-leg table. The whole area is full of splashes of color and personal treasures. This room lifts my spirit.

From here I can see the bay at a distance, but watching the neighborhood is just as intriguing. Herman, our spoiled seagull, sits on the picket fence while I tidy the room. He is, no doubt, looking for a handout. He certainly knows I'm good for at least one feeding a day. Murry was visiting and commented, "What a fat seagull!"

Umbrellas collect on the potting shed's checkered floor. A little desk with a bright-red drawer keeps our flower seeds dry.

We have dinners on the deck all through the month of July. And, of course, they must be by candlelight. On the north porch, a basket of red begonias greets our friends who join us.

I took a long walk down the shore this afternoon. Some waterfront shacks still line the beach as reminders of a long-ago lifestyle when the courageous zealots of Seattle challenged Puget Sound with their small boats and limited skills. They would bring their families to these parts, jettison enough food for a week, and live in one of these little shacks for their entire vacation. The tiny real estate holdings have long since been abandoned, but the shacks still intrigue me. Some have been remodeled by the new owners.

In July, Ron and I love to sleep outdoors. The only sound comes from the changing or retreating of the tide and an occasional stripe-tailed visitor from the forest.

Geese fly by on reconnaissance flights daily. It's their way of building up their youngsters for the long migratory trip back home to Siberia. That's still a ways off, but the regulated flights continue, regardless.

I would live in the outdoor garden rooms year round if I could. Our garden rooms are private places and are becoming more developed every day. Among our favorites are the hydrangea room, the picnic-table room, the eagle's table, and the 'Bloodgood' maple garden.

The woodland garden features a mixed grouping of hemlocks, cedars, firs, and even chestnut trees and provides a walk in the woods like none other. The ground cover is as interesting as the canopy of trees. We have Oregon grape, giant ferns, snowdrops, and false Solomon's seal. The garden is carpeted with white trillium blossoms that turn pinkish with age. Oxalis, also known as redwood sorrel, forms a sea of clover. It's a garden that feeds the soul.

The picnic-table garden room, of course, features the table that washed up on our beach. We have had many guests join us there for candlelight dinners, but breakfast meals are the most popular. We pull out the Coleman stove and cook bacon and scrambled eggs with cheese and blueberry pancakes. We use our camp coffee pot to brew coffee. Our outdoor breakfast wafts through the woods.

July 2

Ten-year old Logan just rode passed on his bicycle all by himself; I'm sure he's going to the country meat market. He has a thing for beef jerky and the store makes some of the finest. We wave to each other.

I see Mel, who's nearly one hundred years old, ride by on his bicycle. Mel is a fixture in town. Everybody knows him. He says his secret to a long and happy life is, "I'm always thanking God that I've done so well." Yes, you have, Mel. And our whole town has taken notice. Tonight I'll have Logan help me take a meal to him.

July 4

For the holiday, Ron and I made raspberry shortcake to share with five families in our immediate neighborhood. We whipped up fresh cream and sported a raspberry atop each creamy pile. The front door fragrance was the sweet smell of Daphne Odora.

Our children's garden is a favorite: fuzzy Lamb's Ear, Fried Eggs, scented geranium, chocolate mint, spearmint, rosemary and lavender. They touch the senses. Even the worms are popular with the kids.

July 5

The smell of the evergreens in the air is like Christmas. Little hummingbirds, which I call Tinker Bells, have left their nest. It was sunny today, and they were flying through the spray of my garden hose. We savored fresh red snapper for dinner at our Italian restaurant.

July 8

Several weeks ago, Ron predicted good fortune for me when he said, "Suzy, you will have dragonflies in your future." I remember that so vividly because Ron knows I love dragonflies. I always have. I first fell in love with them as a kid, entranced with their multilevel translucent wings and their multifaceted eyes. Well, today, while I was taking a walk in a nearby island park, sitting on a bench, a dragonfly landed on my shoulder. Sometimes you just wonder what nature knows that it's not telling. I just hope that special messenger isn't dinner for an unsympathetic frog tonight.

July 11

I woke up this morning and opened the front door to find a deer lying just outside as though he were our pet dog.

We purchased another flat of raspberries on the island. While Ron was cleaning the roof gutters and washing windows, I made two batches of raspberry jam. What raspberries we didn't eat and jam, we put on a tray for the freezer.

Jill's grandfather lived to be over 100 years old. He told everyone his long life was because of Jill's homemade raspberry jam.

We celebrated the day's events with a lunch date.

July 14

It's a beautiful day. Ron is due home from Texas in a few days. My niece Margot visited from east of Seattle. She's such an accomplished writer. I was intrigued with a quote she gave from Sir Philip Sidney: "I think (and I think I think rightly)."

July 16

It's partly cloudy, perfect for sitting outdoors with iced tea. I walked through the woods on the island. The yellow-jacket was asleep again in the foxglove. I picked three more boxes of those addictive raspberries. *Restrain yourself, Susan.* I gave two of the boxes to Cindy. Then I lazed around all day.

July 17

Enough with the raspberries—it's time to write! I spent most of the day at my computer, but I thought about raspberries.

July 18

I dropped Ron off at the ferry dock. He's off to Dallas—or is it Milwaukee this time?—but will be back in a couple of days. That will give me a little time to plan a special party in his honor. I'm always amazed at the stories he brings home: stories of the Minnesota beauty, or Arizona's desert charm, or the glitz of Broadway, or the beaches of Miami. But he says he wouldn't trade our world for anyone else's.

The weather has turned cooler, so I worked out by the dahlias, gardening. Later I took a long walk along the beach and near a woodlands garden.

July 21

It's Ron's birthday, so I made his favorite: a homemade, old-fashioned Hershey's chocolate cake with chocolate cream cheese frosting. Research tells us, reports Sandra Boynton, that "fourteen out of any ten individuals like chocolate!"

Wendy and Rich stopped by on jet skis. Kathy and Louis came by boat. Jeff, Spencer, and Kristen came past on water skis. Scott and Patty came over by rowboat. It looked as though we'd turned our waterfront yard into a marina.

July 22

I made cookies today. This is the second day the weather has turned sunny and warm. We had waffles and bacon for lunch. Dan and Helen took us to dinner.

July 24

More heat! To beat it, I hopped a ferry at 9:30 a.m. and had lunch on the waterfront. I picked up Ron after I got back to the island. We had time to share a mocha at the market.

The creatures that visit my garden include: the kingfisher—a jewel-like bird with arrow-like flight. He's a ruddy chestnut, turquoise, and subtle green color. But don't let the sophisticated charm and the Woody Woodpecker silhouette fool you. He's all fisherman—and he's a king at it. He climbs to heights of thirty feet or more, levels off like a helicopter, then, when he's ready, he dives like a thunderbolt, demonstrating laser-like accuracy.

Speaking of woodpeckers, the bullet-nosed specialists are also part of our tree-trunk traffic. More than most, they seem to defy the laws of physics. For starters, using their toes, they climb trees while in an upright position. Their hammer-like beaks will find a suspect spot in a tree, and then the fun begins. They can stroke a spot at a rate of eight times per second—all at a speed of thirteen miles an hour. The shock absorber in their head never seems to wear out.

The hummingbird is perhaps the most social of all the wildlife. These birds want to be included in anything I'm involved with. If I'm gardening, they're there. If I'm filling the birdbaths, suddenly water sports are their favorite game. If I'm in the kitchen fixing a meal, they watch from the window, wondering what I'm doing. If I try to nap on my outside daybed, they're amazed at how I tire so quickly. I'm convinced that every hummingbird is an extrovert. And I love them all!

Jerry, a local fireman, has this poem posted in his garden along the road where I take walks.

Smell the Flowers
Don't hurry and don't worry,
Life's too precious to be rushed.
Take time to hear the blackbird sing
When the evening is hushed.
Don't stumble and don't grumble,
We're only here a while,
So, smell the flowers on your way,
Enjoying every mile.

Don't groan a lot, or moan a lot,
Or dwell on stress and strife,
But see the wonders of the world
And all the gifts of life.
Don't hurry and don't worry,
Enjoy the sun and showers,
We're here for such a little while—
Take time to smell the flowers.

—Iris Hesselden

August

*B*esides hosting bears, cougars, deer, pheasants, eagles, geese, ducks, kingfishers, otters, seals, sandpipers, and owls, we have a creek for salmon. Ferns and trees hang over the creek as it flows into our bay. It's not really our creek, but we enjoy the wildlife gathering at the fresh water. Its official name is Bjorgen Creek.

I'll never forget when we first moved into our cottage by the sea. Early one morning, perhaps four or five o'clock, Ron woke me and said, "What are those sounds? Cats?" The sounds weren't familiar to us, and they went on and on. Then I laughed and said, "Seagulls." These social birds actually band together and form gull colonies. They can live up to twenty years and return to the same place each year after their migration. Little did we know we would gain a pet seagull that we would name Scoop. He has one web missing from his foot. We've known him for ten years now. Then there are Max and Matilda. Max looks like Baby Huey. His offspring have profiles just like his.

When Ron and I were transferred for a short stint, I was amazed to discover that of all the sounds of wildlife, I missed the calls of the seagulls the most.

How can I tell everything about August? There are spinster sisters and their secret garden—oh, and their prophetic words at breakfast in our cottage!

There's the "Alice in Wonderland" mole who tried to undermine a tree at water's edge. And there's life along a fence that watches us.

Where do I begin?

August 1

This morning I was writing in the potting shed's porch when I saw a mother deer and her fawn on our lawn. Mother was teaching her baby. They went to get a drink of saltwater in the bay for their natural quest for sodium.

August 2

I had to call the fire department when a blaze ignited in the old oil stove. The stove was condemned that very day, so we got a beautiful new brown enamel free-standing stove made in France. The whole neighborhood loves that little stove.

August 3

I cleaned leaves from the gutter and found another squid deposited there.

On my daily walk, I stopped in to visit Mrs. Peters, our legally blind neighbor. I think she appreciates the company, because as I was leaving, she offered me a teacup-and-saucer set that dates back to the Civil War. Needless to say, I couldn't accept it, but it speaks well of her generous hospitality.

August 8

Tonight was an art party with neighbors at Wendy's house so we could showcase our stamp art. I created a Christmas town with multiple stamps.

It is hard to sleep tonight because it is so warm. Venus and Saturn are showing off.

Two friends, both six and both named Madeline played with their sand buckets in front of our house. They made me laugh. Their drama and antics. . . beach life is serious at age six.

August 10

Dan and Helen stopped in. Later, wanting cool weather, Ron and I went chasing clouds. We found them. The temperature dropped twenty degrees as we headed toward the mountains. It was invigorating, rejuvenating. Ron took a plastic bag and wore it like a vest. The rain was steady. We tromped through the woods. Creeks were flowing. The smells were fresh.

August 12

I'm writing late tonight, so I made another pot of coffee.

August 14

Our swamp plant—commonly known as "marsh mallow"—thrives near the saltwater. It's in full bloom with large pink hollyhock blossoms. In olden days, they made marshmallows from this plant. It's aptly named.

Picked blackberries all morning and have blackberry stains all over my fingers and probably between my teeth as well. I'll make Aunt Mabel's blackberry cobbler.

Eleven guys in suits were eating lunch at one picnic table designed to seat six in town today.

I also took a walk on the beach. I love inspecting the shanties on the shore. They hold fishing gear, kayaks, and occasionally boats. I'd love to sleep on the water's edge some night.

I picked twenty purple magnolias and am floating them in a large bowl.

Squirrels have been carrying our green tomatoes to the top of the garden shed where they ripen in the sunshine. I told Aunt Mabel, my centenarian gardening expert, that the squirrels were harvesting my crop. She said, "Squirrels are supposed to collect nuts." I guess I caught her off guard by answering, "These squirrels are nuts." She let out a good, deep laugh.

Aunt Mabel, 101 years old, lives in Tipton, Missouri. She has the same flowers in her Midwest garden that I have in my Northwest garden. She told me the order in which her flowers bloom. She announced, "The blooming order is crocus, daffodil, tulip, iris, poppy, peony, daylily, mum, cannas, *and then frost."*

Thankful is not strong enough to describe the joy of living in our little beach cottage. I'm overwhelmed, elated, ecstatic, savoring every moment of this treasured life.

August 20

I enjoyed a dinner of cod with Marcy and Lance.

August 21

It's cooler! I made an old-fashioned chocolate cake and took some to the Best family with their four children. I baked granola chocolate-chip cookies too. Kayaks and rowboats are out tonight.

August 23

Visited a small tea shop this morning and bought Devonshire cream. I made a fire in the fire pit tonight. I saw two shooting stars zigzag across the sky.

August 24

Picked up Jenn and Katie, two sisters from Idaho. We had lunch at the cottage, and then I got them back on the ferry.

Wildlife watches us out of the bushes and brambles. I catch them looking while I garden. It's as if they want to get involved. A chipmunk just peeked at me from around the corner of the deck. Hummingbirds are buzzing me. And the squirrels are curious too. I heard the owl this morning again.

And as in dreams, I wrap this land
Around me as a shawl. The heady green of everywhere-trees,
Have sponged away the years, the tears
And
Brought my heart to ease.
Beneath the cloudy skies my
Childhood memories call. . . .
I wrap this land around me like a shawl.
—Phyllida Miller

The hummingbird fight unhinged all the other birds, and it went on for several days. Some days you need an air traffic controller. The yellow jackets are sleeping in the hollyhocks.

August 27

There's an old picnic basket full of various mints along the kitchen path: chocolate mint, orange mint, licorice mint, as well as dill and cilantro. What a lunchbox! Quite often I find a little green frog in there too.

I love the sixteen-year-old azalea a friend found and planted for us. He lost his sunglasses in the process, but we found them in the mulch a year later.

Today my clothesline is literally afloat in the breeze with sheets, pillowcases, and towels. I remember hearing a story titled "Clotheslines" by Charles Kuralt. It was about people's love of their clotheslines. Mine is a mainstay in my life.

August 30

The two spinster sisters invited me for dinner in their 1910 cabin next door. You can't see the cabin because it's so overgrown with apple trees, pear trees, hawthorn trees, and who knows what else? Their parents owned the property before they did, and they are both in their eighties.

Before I met the sisters, I saw them picking our softball-sized 'King' apples. The huge fruit makes incredible pies. The sisters even knew where to find our apple picker, a long pole with a catcher's mitt on the end. They informed me that they had always picked apples on our property, and this was a tradition. That was fine with me.

But where did they live? Well, next door, I discovered! They showed me a little trail that led into the woods. I followed them until it opened to a cleared swatch of tomatoes, rhubarb, chard, and cucumbers. I named it the "Secret Garden".

I returned the favor of dinner at their cabin with breakfast at our cottage. They came in the back door that morning and said, "This is always the way we come in." They left later through the front door. June remarked, "When visitors come in the back and leave out the front, it means you're going to have lots of company."

And she was right. From then on, I began to pay attention to the constant drop-ins. After that, we named our place the drive-through cottage.

Today my wildlife challenge was a mole who was trying to undermine a tree. We tried everything but couldn't trap it. He came out just when the sun was going down. Ron was gone, and I knew I had to be the one to catch or kill the critter. I was barefoot and watched him go across our yard for about fifteen feet, squirming and squiggling. Then, talking to myself, I observed, "He is going to undermine your whole house if you don't do something, Susan."

So I went to the garage and got a shovel. I approached him slowly as he showed his two buck teeth. Finally I summoned the courage to whack him over the head with the shovel. *Eeeeeekkkkk!*

Then I remembered a game of croquet in *Alice in Wonderland*. What did they use for a croquet ball? Yep, a gopher. Wanna come to my house and play croquet?

It is the last day of August, and we hit a record at eighty-eight degrees. But it did rain, and two kingfishers and I celebrated. They stretched and turned and opened their beaks to drink up the rain.

September

S eptember is a first in many ways: school starts, the weather
changes, and nature begins the long preparation for winter.

Early this morning, an otter on the beach held a big salmon in
its mouth. Suddenly an eagle swooped down and the commotion
began. The otter and eagle fought mightily over that salmon. Guess
who won? The otter flipped the salmon into the water, and both
eagle and otter dove for it. With much splashing of water, the pursuit
ensued. Then suddenly the victor showcased its spoils, and the eagle
flew away with the big fish.

"It takes courage just to up and say you don't like the country,"
wrote Lillian Hellmann in the 1906 *American Writer.* "Everybody
likes the country."

September 2

This morning, while writing at my desk, I heard barking on the
beach. Kathy was down by the water putting a leash on her dog. But
upon closer inspection I noticed it wasn't the dog barking but a large
sea lion positioned just off shore. Kathy informed me that the sea
lion who is known as Big Boy is infamous for his cunning ability
to find food, whether it be fish, fowl or canine. During lean times,
when the fish are few, Big Boy has been known to coax dogs off the
shore and into the water where it's not a fair fight. Big Boy surfaces
when the salmon are running. And it's for this reason that many
homeowners carefully monitor their dog's daily walks.

September 4

I did the wash and got it onto the clothesline. I also aired out the goose-down comforter and pillows.

I talked to several neighbors and walked along the bay for close to an hour. I met another neighbor and chatted about buying their old woodstove.

I went to the local market and looked at flowers. For lunch, I bought the lunch special: the best French dip sandwich!

Blackberries were ripe for the picking on the beach. I also bought tulip and daffodil bulbs and a new shovel, and then planted some things with the neighbor boy. Another neighbor boy asked if he could mow our lawn for me. Little boys *smell*!

September 7

Watering, fertilizing. . . summer days are racing by. Eric, a neighbor boy, and I found one hundred bulbs and lots of challenging rocks. We're calling this the "rock and bulb garden." We ate raspberries atop vanilla-bean ice cream.

Tall firs and broad cedars are bending at their crests. The winds have picked up; a sure sign that fall is on the way. And, if there was any doubt, the maples' leaves are turning golden.

It's September, so the pears, plums, apples, and grapes are producing their fruit.

Ron and I identify with Rick Bass as he let loose with his emotions in *Winter*: "Elizabeth and I feel as though we have fallen into heaven. We have stumbled into the pie!"

The best way to get a good garden is to stuff it.
—Vita Sackville West

Our woods are stuffed with wood-sorrel oxalis. Their leaves are heart shaped and look like shamrocks. From the lily family, we have false Solomon's seal. They sport whitish berries speckled with brown. Our liver-red trillium is also from the lily family.

Bramble blackberries and giant ferns abound. When the deer foot fern unfurled its leaves it looks just like a deer's foot. Holly, Oregon grape, salmonberries, and a giant viburnum all love the cool woods.

September 10

Today I'm planting several trees. Ron and I found a great sale. One of the trees is a Linden tree. It's a great shade tree. I know just where I'll put it.

I can vaguely see the ferryboat down the channel. It's crossing from our peninsula past an island, heading toward the city. Its bright, white lights serve as an attention-getter as much as a pathfinder. But the angle limits my vision. If I blink, I'll miss the show.

A red seaplane just landed across the bay. It appears to be picking up some passengers. My mind imagines they're flying off to dinner to some remote, potbelly diner.

The loons are close on our beach. Though I can't see them, I can hear their call. By this time of year, the young loons have learned to swim and have climbed down from the safety of their parents' backs. It's one of the great pictures of nature.

September 14

I'll be writing tonight. Even though Ron's out of town, I have had too many distractions to get much done.

September 16

It's Sunday morning, and little black ducks have been playing tag for hours. Later I'll wade out onto the beach to see if that injured starfish is still there and to see whether he's all right. I have to be careful. Mr. Starfish lives in the dangerous quicksand. These are my new boots, and I'd rather not sacrifice them to Davy Jones's locker. I've already lost one pair to the legend of the sea.

I put a pot of bulbs together and dug a hole in the garden for it. On December 15, I'll pull the pot out of the ground to force the bulbs to bloom early indoors. Let's see, I'm planting 'Red Apeldorn' tulips, 'Passionale' daffodils with their white petals and contrasting pink trumpets, crocus, snowdrops, butterfly narcissus, and of course 'King Alfred' daffodils.

Last summer when my college roommate visited, we explored sea life together. We saw a giant sea snail sucking on a clam the size of a starfish. In my excitement, I hadn't noticed that I was heading straight toward some small sinkholes. Sure enough, I landed dead center in one of them and soon was up to my knees in a hole of watery sand. Bent over on all fours, I became stuck. The harder my friend pulled on my leg, the harder we laughed. Soon our hysterics filled the beach with laughter, like the bark of a boisterous sea lion. It took all the strength two laughing women had to pry my foot loose and then say good-bye to a good pair of boots.

September 19

Today the entire beach is quiet, with everyone gone back to school or to their usual routines. Once again, sea life and birds of the air rule this splendid kingdom.

I never dreamed that a chickadee would land in my hand to eat sunflower seeds. His little feet on my skin felt so funny.

> Let your boat of life be light,
> Packed with only what you need—a homely home
> Simple pleasures, one or two friends worth the name
> Someone to love and someone to love you,
> A cat, a dog, and a pipe or two, enough to eat and
> Enough to wear, and a little more than enough to drink
> For thirst is a dangerous thing.
> —Jerome Klapka Jerome

September 22

As I was driving to town to run some errands, a gust of wind blew, and all of a sudden a barrage of colorful leaves swept over my car as if to announce the first day of fall. Swoosh!

It's cloudy and misty, a perfect time to plant. So out came the shovel and down went twenty-five seedling trees we received from Dan's tree storage. Dan and Helen are some of our oldest friends. Dan has a heart for seedlings. He'll scour his property for seedlings, dig them up, and plant them in his tree storage, a twenty-by-thirty-feet area that allows the little green sprigs a higher survival rate. He asks us to take as many as we can, so we do.

Today I missed my dad, a resident of heaven now for twenty years. In his honor, I made his favorite: a far-out navy recipe called 'zee' stuff on d'shingle (tomato sauce on toast). It's delicious. Thanks, Dad.

September 25
Thundershowers watered the earth last night, but I picked apples this morning. Wendy came by in her little putt-putt boat and asked me to hop in. We sailed off to town for a cup of hot coffee.

September 26
The farmers' market happens every Wednesday down at the marina. It's tough to resist the bounty of the sea and the gardens. But today I spent my wad on fresh fruit and veggies—strawberries, parsley, chives, beets, and zucchini. By that time, I was in the mood to bake. So bran muffins and onion-dill bread became delights du jour. I even made some cinnamon rolls for Nancy and Murry. On my way to deliver them, I found an anonymous bouquet of flowers on my back porch. It proved the old adage "one good turn deserves another." Next farmers' market, I will be sure to buy kettle corn.

My suspicion is that the freshly picked flowers were a gift from the Harvey girls, two preteens who grow flowers in their backyard and sell them from their driveway flower stand. You just leave your money in a jar.

One day when I saw them riding their bikes, I complained, "Everyone buys your flowers before I get there!"

"Oh," they replied, "we'll bring some to your house."

Not long afterward, two bicycles came down the driveway, hauling two huge bouquets for me. The two young girls came in for a while and were a bubble of fun. For an hour they sat on my double-rocking chair as we discussed their favorite sights and sounds of nature and the books they most enjoyed. "Suzy," they said as they were about to leave, "you must watch *Ann of Avonlea* on television tonight." So I did.

Geese fill the beach with laughter now. I saw seven baby geese and seven teenaged geese this morning. They talk incessantly, but I can't get enough of their conversations. The only other sound seems to be coming from the chipmunks, the busy, boisterous citizens of our community.

Last night a raccoon found a bucket of clams I forgot to bring into the garage. He shucked them as fast as I can shuck an ear of corn. Then he flung the shells all over the lawn. So tomorrow it's back to digging, if I'm ever going to make homemade chowder or clam linguine for company.

Sunsets at this time of year are painfully beautiful. Seagulls in flight parallel the shore and complete the scene. Waves lap quietly upon the beach. All is right with the world.

Tomorrow will be another minus tide. I hope to find signs of geoduck clams on the beach, those curious types that leave the largest air holes and fill the biggest soup tureen.

At the country meat market, I bought some apple sausage. I plan to make sausage-and-white-bean soup. It sticks to your ribs. Of course, that means I'll have to make cottage-cheese biscuits to dunk in the broth. Garlic cloves and red wine complete the meal of savory soup.

Skeletons of red crabs, eaten by the birds, are strewn on footpaths. It looks as though it's been a good day for all of us dwellers by the beach—all except the clams and crabs, that is.

Today we are spreading twelve yards of bark on our property. Rhododendrons, azaleas, and peonies, however, don't like bark at their feet.

"Larceny of time and mind" is what Emily Dickinson called the mundane chores required of her. Ms. Dickinson and I have a lot in common. I'd rather write or take in wildlife and nature than do just about anything else.

The kingfisher is diving off the Pacific madrone tree into the water today. Flocks of geese are visible in the distance, coaxing their young to strengthen their wings for the long migratory flight ahead. I miss them already. I think I'll go to bed early tonight.

Outside, twilight is falling.
And there's a chill in the air.
The moon shimmers in the misty sky,
But inside the lights are low, the fire is cozy.
—Author unknown

To everything there is a season: a time to plant. . . a time to heal. . .
a time to dance. . .
—Ecclesiastes 3

October

I love October days. Summer walkers that earlier populated the
beach are now gone, "leaving the sand to true beach lovers who
have a more long-term relationship with the sea," as someone once
said. So, for us locals, this is our time of year, and we can feel the
snap in the air. But I have to refocus! It's time to get our rustic wood
table ready for a Thanksgiving party seaside style.

The leaves can fall while I stuff squash and apples into a
cleaned-out pumpkin, while in the background the pretty multicolored sweet peas fill a vase. Yellow flowers and red berries adorn
the Saint-John's-wort. And outside, baby seagulls are still nagging
their mothers for food. But it won't be long before their feathers will
thicken and they'll be on their own to find their own meals. Mean-
time, I'm busy picking fresh corn and cleaning potatoes freshly dug
from the ground.

This is autumn, with its multicolored and polka-dot leaves that
will soon be gathered and pressed inside large books.

Mornings are cold and wet, contrasting the sunny and dry after-
noons. The Harvey girls, who are now in school, still found time
to set up their flower stand and are selling the last of the season's
dahlias along the roadside. I'm thinking a bunch of their dahlias
would look great with some new geraniums I bought, which reminds
me, I need to plant the 'Pink Diamond' tulip bulbs before the ground
gets too hard to dig. Oh well, maybe another day. For now, it's cozy
inside as the furnace heats the house.

Our neighbor's trees are full of plums and stone-hard pears. It makes me want to make pear tartlets today. Or maybe I'll make apple pie, since the 'King' apple tree is burdened with an extra-heavy load.

All throughout the yard, the mums are splashing their burgundy, yellow, and hot-pink beauty. But even they will be gone before long as we prepare for the colder months.

It's during this time of year that I most love to take walks, or, as I tend to call them, "treasure hunts." You just never know what you're going to find in fall.

I collected fall leaves to put under my glass tabletop. I also picked apples and miniature pink roses at the secret garden next door where the spinster sisters live. I just filled a pewter vase with 'Viking' mums, colored leaves, and orange berries. I placed a basket of fall leaves, apples, and pears on our English gate-leg table.

Our mud porch is our savior. A basket of apples, some boots, shoes, jackets, and umbrellas line the wall.

Black-eyed Susans are on display. Their chocolate button centers make me want to eat them.

The common mullein came up by itself. The flower is from the snapdragon family, but ours gets six feet tall. The flannel-textured leaves are stunning.

I'm reminded that Halloween is near when I see a dark-black crow eating bright-orange pyracantha berries. Orange and black. . . hmmm. . .

October 1

Last night a neighbor dad and his small son peeked into our front window while Ron and I were having pizza for dinner. When I saw the ghoulish faces and Halloween costumes, my first thought was that I'd had too much pepperoni. But thankfully, it was just Jeff and Spencer giving us a Halloween preview. Spencer kept looking through the window for our usual bowl of Hershey kisses that he's grown so fond of. But Jeff, a business owner in Seattle, kept looking at the pizza. Luckily for Spencer, he left a happy boy, with Hershey chocolate stuffed in his cheeks, and Jeff left with a large slice of pizza heaped with all the pepperoni I could put on it. I felt it was my best insurance against seeing any more scary faces that night, whether through my window or in my dreams.

October 2

I set the alarm for 4:00 a.m. and wrote all day. A ball of fluff called a baby hawk took a bath at daybreak, holding its breath and then plunging headfirst into our fountain. A windstorm stirred both our community and our emotions, but I wrote on.

My neighbors and I picked 'King' apples off the ground from our hundred-year-old tree. They were the size of softballs. We made a four-pound winter-apple pie. Winter has started early. Our furnace ran all day for the first time in quite a while.

October 3

The morning began with a heavy cloud cover and the beginning of rain.

October 5

A few light showers fell. As the day progressed, I had lunch out with a friend, ran errands to the bank and the cleaners, and then dropped off a manuscript at the post office. After working on reunion scrapbooks, I lost myself in the memories of college.

October 7

Today was another partly sunny–very foggy morning. But I refused to succumb to the temptation to stay indoors. Instead, I challenged myself to walk to Patty's with a backpack full of pot roast and mixed veggies. Patty and I found baby Benjamin quite a handful.

Tonight I prepared butternut squash for the freezer.

October 10

It's rainy and windy, with the sun appearing late. I made bean soup and beef stock.

October 13

Surprise! Today is unusually warm. And making the day even brighter, I received a book from Katie.

Rhododendrons have started to bloom. I was digging around my favorite rhodie, 'Mrs. Furnival', and accidentally sat on her. Oops! Another favorite rhodie of mine is 'Sappho', with its white flowers and dramatic dark-purple blotch. 'Red Walloper' is incredible too. But 'Belle Heller', a white with gold blotches, is truly an award winner.

October 18

It looks as though we're going to have an Indian summer. Our sunrise in cool weather was beautiful.

October 20

Well, so much for the Indian summer! It was cold when I rose at 6:00 a.m., but the day grew quite warm by noon. With a long-handled brush and garden hose, I cleaned out the birdbaths. I'm convinced the birds were thankful.

October 24

It appears today will be much cooler, which is perfect for my ferry ride at 10:15 a.m. I'm going to the city for a surprise visit with Margaret and Scott.

October 27

Neighbor Dan made a new garden bench for us. He fashioned it from a photo of an old craftsman's bench from an English Tudor home in northern California. I knew Dan was up to the challenge, but I had no idea he was such an artisan. The garden bench looks exactly like the one in the photo. I celebrated by making stew and a loaf of bread for dinner.

October 28

Today was mostly sunny, but cooler. Fall is definitely here. Niece Margot came to visit with one express purpose: to venture through a local corn maze at a nearby farm. What we didn't expect was all the other activities available: picking dahlias, petting llamas, going on hayrides, drinking hot chocolate, gathering apples, and launching pumpkins towards a well-marked target in the next pasture. What fun!

October 30

I could tell that something outside was different. No birds risked flight. Then the wind started howling and continued all day. Inside, I made popcorn balls for trick-or-treaters.

October 31

During the hailstorm, poor Murry had to finish his new picket fence. As if by cruel irony, the weather turned nice just as he finished. And soon the first goblins began to arrive, right about sundown.

During all the rain and hail of the past two days, the fall leaves, which were primed to come down soon anyway, all took flight at the same time. And there it was—the entire ground, road, and lawns a multicolored mosaic of seasonal leaves resembling a massive quilt spread. No wonder fall is my favorite season.

November

*P*umpkin patches are all the rage this time of year. They spring up in the most nondescript places: open fields, school ball-yards, and church parking lots—just everywhere. I doubt there's a store in the county that doesn't have a stacked display of the bright orange balls blocking a portion of their parking lot.

I couldn't believe my eyes today when I saw two pumpkins bobbing in the water along our seashore. My initial knee-jerk reaction told me they were buoys. Buoys are a mainstay for all the boats in our bay. Even though the boats are corralled for the winter, the buoys are tied to a sunken anchor and left out to bob in the water all winter long.

Slipping on my big boots and staying clear of the quicksand, I made my way down the beach. And there they were—not buoys at all, but pumpkins, each weighing about ten pounds, I would guess.

I love the bounty of the sea, even when it's a sea imposter. This is going to be a good and tasty November.

November 1

I put our 'King' apples on the eagles' dinner table, but today they're all gone. The table is an old tree stump about the same diameter as our own dining table, and the eagles frequent their table about as often as we do ours. Skeletons were left behind, as were half a dozen seashells.

November 2
It was a dark morning and stayed that way all day. Squirrels have been burying things. One stopped on the deck and looked at me with a pinecone in its mouth—just showing off, no doubt.

November 5
Today was mostly sunny, but crisp. I went for a country walk. Rich and Wendy invited us to dinner. In the center of the table was a giant platter of pasta with the aroma of basil, garlic and oregano.

November 6
I transplanted some fir and cedar trees. I stopped at the post office to mail a manuscript to an editor.

November 7
Sharp frost covered the ground. I voted today. I also made home-made burritos, cooking the sauce all day. Jeff and Debbie saw us gardening, so they stopped by — but didn't volunteer to pull any weeds!

November 8
Salmon were jumping, and the weather was stormy. The seagulls and ducks seemed frightened by the huge salmon.

November 9
A heavy rainstorm pelted us this morning.

November 11
Ron spent time in the workshop and pump house. We put Styrofoam on outdoor faucets and covered some plants in case of frost.

November 14
We took the half-hour ferry ride to Seattle to purchase Christmas cards and a few presents. Meanwhile, Ron took off from there for a flight to Los Angeles. He'll be back tomorrow.

November 15
It was below freezing at night. I made stuffed dates with walnuts.
We've had three sets of company so far this month. They came from Georgia and California.

November 17
Our first snow came today. I found myself squealing with the excitement of the weather. I am silly with joy.

November 18
Ron and I headed to the city for the stage show "My Fair Lady". We caught the late ferry home and watched as snow fell the entire

trip. The power was off when we arrived home. But we were too tired to care.

November 20

The broken aggregate for paths around our home came from several sources; the mayor's house, the Presbyterian Church, and a neighbor. Fifteen workers laid the aggregate path during a hailstorm. Meanwhile Ron and I baked some bread with loads of butter between the slices and delivered it to the guys.

In the spring we'll plant Corsican mint and wooly thyme between the stepping-stones.

Squirrels keep busy burying things. One squirrel found some building insulation and added it to an abandoned bird feeder to create a winterized home.

November 21

We decided to walk into town on the freshly fallen snow. Our hamlet has never been more beautiful. Later we made squash in a pumpkin and baked our favorite onion-dill bread. With winter on its way, we drained the outdoor shower near the beach. The snow lasted longer than usual today. It was a two–goose-down night.

November 22

I spent the day writing letters. Ron got our car fixed. A driver from the auto shop brought him home. Ron asked the driver, "Would you mind making one stop? I need to pick up a turkey for our Thanksgiving dinner." The man cordially obliged.

November 23

It's Thanksgiving, one of our great American traditions and holidays. Scott, Margaret, and three of their four kids celebrated with us. The kids made a beeline for the indoor swing hanging from the living-room beams; the swing is a whimsical addition to our home.

Our celebratory feast featured turkey, rolls, cranberry relish, ambrosia in frozen orange shells, mashed potatoes and gravy, and three-berry pie and Aunt Mabel's turkey haystack cookies for dessert. And, of course, we enjoyed a favorite tradition of mine: enchiladas, another whimsical addition. After a full day of visiting, card playing, and a shivering walk on the beach, our guests caught the 9:40 p.m. ferry for home—still full, as were we.

Ron and I hopped into the car and drove around our small burg to see how others were celebrating the holiday. Our town loves any excuse to celebrate.

November 26
The air feels as though snow is coming. Church was good. We played in the garden most of the afternoon then ate leftovers from our Thanksgiving dinner: turkey sandwiches on egg bread, cranberry relish, and three-berry pie.

November 28
Everyone seems to have caught the Christmas spirit all at the same time. Christmas lights are everywhere. We packed a thermos of hot tea, along with cheese and crackers, then headed seventeen miles down the waterway. At a certain roadside pullout, we used our binoculars to locate our house and could see its entire roof lined with Christmas lights.

November 29

We raked leaves and then enjoyed fresh fish and Caesar salad for lunch. Not being very hungry, we steamed some vegetables for dinner: chard, cabbage, and brussel sprouts.

November 30

After making Christmas bread, I wrote all day. A sign on our door reads, "Gone to Tea." That night a wild windstorm splashed waves over the bulkhead and onto our lawn. Four huge trees, two cedars and two firs, fell across the length of our property. Thankfully, no damage occurred.

Rain
The rain is raining all around,
It falls on field and tree
It's raining on the umbrellas here
And on the ships at sea.
—Robert Louis Stevenson

December

*O*ne thing remains constant in the Northwest: the weather. There's always plenty of it, and it's always changing.

When I was a girl growing up on the beaches of Southern California, my parents would always tell us kids, "Don't ever turn your back on a wave." The same can be said about our Northwest weather. Don't ever turn your back on it. Don't let it lull you into a false sense of security. But that's exactly what happened last December.

Ron was in Chicago on business, flying home on Monday night. The television weatherman announced we were in the path of an "arctic blast." But those words had no meaning to me. As far as I knew, an arctic blast was a confectionary from the local ice cream truck.

Ron arrived home safely, with tales of a bumpy plane ride and strong winds faced in flight. And sure enough, that night while we attempted to stay warm under three goose-down blankets piled high, the arctic blast came calling.

For the next three days, we lost all electricity and phone service. As a result, we had no running water, no heat, and no way to communicate with the outside world. Fortunately, just fifty yards from the house, we did have a pile of leftover wood stacked high under a fir tree and two feet of snow.

But Ron had fallen victim to a flu bug and was flat on his back, out of commission for most of the blizzard. So I became the pioneer woman.

I stirred up my "witch's brew" for Ron. It's gross, but it really works. Here's the recipe:

1 tablespoon lecithin
1 tablespoon oil
1 tablespoon acidophilus milk
1½ teaspoons calcium lactate
½ teaspoon magnesium
¼ cup soy powder
¼ cup brewer's yeast powder
2 teaspoons vanilla
1 quart pineapple juice

Back and forth to the woodpile I went, stoking the home fire while my Prince Charming moaned under the goose-downs. In retrospect, we must have lived on grilled cheese sandwiches toasted on our wood-burning stove.

If necessity is the mother of invention, then I birthed more than my share of creative efforts that week. Try bathing in a twenty-gallon metal wash bucket or melting snow for drinking water. I'm sure our grandparents did the same thing without hesitation. Between Ron's sickness, candle-power living, and makeshift culinary tricks, our house had a ransacked look in every room.

When Ron could finally get around, I convinced him that a walk into town would be his best cure. I wasn't sure if the cold would make him better or worse, but I knew it would definitely make me better. I had developed an acute case of cabin fever. So we pulled on our snow boots, and off we went.

Nearly every store was closed. They, too, were without power. But we did find one enterprising merchant who'd discovered a way to heat coffee on his river-rock fireplace. That was all Ron and I needed. Together we sat, sipping coffee and munching on potato chips for what seemed like hours. In all that time, not one other customer ventured into the shop. Possibly they were much smarter than we. They probably knew what the words *arctic blast* meant.

On the aesthetic side, I was tugged outdoors by the unimaginably beautiful landscape the winter storm had brought. The sedum

'Autumn Joy' proudly displayed blossoms left over from summer, now serving as podiums for the freshly fallen snow. They looked like lollipops. Snow on the magnolia tree was breathtaking. Our woods, like those of the traveler in Ralph Waldo Emerson's poem "Stopping by Woods on a Snowy Evening," were lovely, dark, and deep. But unlike the traveler in the poem, I didn't have "miles to go before I sleep."

But the town was crippled by the blast. There was no postal service and no cars on the road. Even the city's snowplows were incapacitated.

Every year my husband and I read a book together. A favorite is Lillian Beckwith's *The Sea for Breakfast*. There's nothing like a book, said Ellen Wheeler Wilcox, "to take you lands away."

First a bookcase with a great many books in it;
Next a table that will keep steady when you write or work at it.
Have nothing in your house which you do not know
To be useful or believe to be beautiful.
— William Morris
The Beauty of Life (1880)

Ron and I enjoy making homemade soups, sitting by a cozy fire, and rifling through our library. Reading our books is like spending time with old friends.

Our books range from topics about nature, wildlife, and gardening to science, theology, and history. We have even found in the used bookstores some favorite books from childhood. Angelo Patri said, "Good books are the priceless inheritance of childhood, and no child can be cheated of the legacy without suffering grave spiritual loss."

Ron found the entire set of *The Book of Life* in our bookstore. We love the description of daybreak by Robert Louis Stevenson in one of the volumes:

> In the hedges and whins sleeping birds awaking.
> I am up at the crack of dawn.

I, too, am up at the crack of dawn because I have *Berlinerkranser* to bake. These are Norwegian butter cookies, and making them is a December tradition at our house.

We had a snowstorm that left a canvas of fresh snow. Ron and I hiked to town for coffee. While we were gone, both the Best family with their four kids, and Scott, Patty, and Benjamin all trekked up the hill to our home and found our footprints in the snow going towards town. Sadly we missed each other.

December 1

It's 6:00 a.m. in the morning and the moon is shimmering on the bay. I have candles in each of our cottage windows. I might take a walk later along our winter beach.

Ron is at a convention in Texas. I wrote all day. Snow clouds are overhead. I made myself notes from a well-known phrase:

Don't forget to hang the stockings.

Don't forget Santa's cookies and milk.

Don't forget whose birthday it is.

December 3

At different neighboring farms, we have something called "Christmas in the Country." Arts and crafts are sold, and breads and pastries are in abundance. Spinning wool hats and scarves is a generational tradition at a local farm. Then there's breakfast at another long-term family enterprise, where an old farmhouse serves up homemade baked goods, soups, and any number of mouthwatering temptations. We had apple sausage, blueberry pancakes, and freshly squeezed orange juice.

Another tradition in our home is to buy a live four-to-five-feet-tall Christmas tree, complete with its root-ball. Then we sink it into a large garden pot and place the entire display in a sleigh we picked up from the hardware store. Some years earlier, the town challenged all the local stores to showcase their storefront windows with a seasonal display, with a prize awarded for the best display. Our hardware store won top honors with the cutest red-and-green sleigh, big enough for both Ron and me to climb into. We were fortunate to be the first to ask to buy it, and today it graces our front porch. Stuffed inside the sleigh are brightly wrapped packages, a large Santa bag tied with a rope, and a beautifully lit Christmas tree.

December 4

We have a recipe box with an index card titled "Christmas" written in red letters. I made Christmas cookies, Hungarian nut rolls, and cream-cheese wreaths. I baked pecan rolls and orange rolls. Outside, a stiff wind is blowing.

Today's to-do list consists of the following: Type, trim giant ferns, and transplant some baby trees. Get the furnace checked, and bring in the outdoor furniture, including the daybed. Bake bread.

December 5

The wind knocked down some tree branches. High tides add to the danger. I decide to batten down the hatches.

I brought in my last cut rose, 'Cologne', to protect it from the frost. The fragrance was a long reminder of the past rose season.

I fed the birds, and then a couple of dozen flew out of the garden. Hundreds of ducks are feeding on smelt. I try to enjoy these slow times. They are gifts. God forbid that I should walk through this beautiful world with unseeing eyes.

December 8

Ron worked on notes for a speaking engagement. During the day, the neighborhood was buzzing with news of a black bear surveying the neighborhood. It's common practice to warn anyone living nearby of these marvelous but dangerous beasts. Unbeknownst to us, our friend Patty was out on her daily walk with a stroller carrying her twin baby girls. From one of the houses along the treed drive came the words, "Watch out for the bear!" Patty couldn't tell where the voice was coming from but knew to get home as soon as possible. We felt bad we weren't there to offer her a ride. Thankfully, everything turned out well. Later that night, we saw the bear crossing the road about a mile from our home.

December 9

"Hear ye, hear ye; come one, come all." Little Norway has thirty caroling groups all competing for the annual reign as Musical Group of the Year. Each group huddles along Main Street and sings their heart out. A bucket for contributions is placed in front of each group, and a dollar bill represents a vote. Ron and I got a handful of ones and dropped a vote into each bucket. All the proceeds go to benefit a food bank. While the adults were casting their ballots, families climbed aboard the horse-drawn carriage for free rides through downtown.

December 10

I heard my first loon today. As I got him focused in my binoculars, I saw the biggest eagle hassling the loon and a nearby duck. Each time the eagle would dive for them, the loon and the duck would dive underwater.

I had a snow tea party for the neighborhood children. I served cream puffs and peach tea. Little signs on the table said, "I ♥ snow."

December 12

We planted 250 daffodil bulbs. Ice made driving on the roads dangerous. The birdbath froze over. Soon a weather emergency was broadcast, warning that a blizzard was on its way. Although it lasted only a few days, it left an imprint upon my mind.

December 17

We had showers, followed by a few snowflakes. The weather was clear but cold. A wise woman once said, "The divine moment is the present moment."

Ron bought me an early Christmas gift; a bright red wheelbarrow. That was the only color available. Later, when Aunt Mabel called from Missouri, I complained to her, "I don't want to draw attention to myself in the garden with this big red wheelbarrow."

"Oh," she retorted, "you should want people to know you're a gardener."

But I replied, "I'm a private gardener."

December 18

Today was a contractor's delight. Brea and Logan came over, and together we constructed a gingerbread house. The design was complete with frosting for a snowy landscape. Brea found a miniature For Sale sign in my top desk drawer, a holdover from my real estate days, and planted it right in front of the new construction. Logan then said, "And today is open house," and quickly took a bite right out of the roof.

December 19

This morning we caught the ferry to go Christmas shopping and were greeted with sporadic snowflakes.

Tonight we built a bonfire to greet the Christmas boat parade that passes by all our homes. Santa Claus rode through town on top of the fire truck, tossing candy to kids in their neighborhoods.

December 22

It was an icy morning. A seal climbed onto our float, it was slippery. A bird tried to take a bath but went sliding across the birdbath's ice. You could hear the sound of strong branches in nearby fir trees cracking.

This is the Great Northwest. An older man cut the waters cleanly in his handmade canoe as he glided past my house on this record-cold day. There was not a cloud left in the sky. Loons, ducks, and blue heron were out. That night two river otters swam by in the moonlight on the bay.

December 23

We wrapped gifts and prepared the turkey and cranberry relish. Ron made homemade eggnog. I stuffed Christmas treats into a new pair of red-and-yellow rain boots, hung stockings indoors on a clothesline, and decorated the tree with apples and candles.

We picked up rugulah and three-berry pie on a nearby island for our dinner guests.

We are having peppermint shakes in champagne glasses with a peppermint stick in each glass. A candle will be clamped onto everyone's Christmas plate, and a framed photo of each family member will identify the place settings.

December 25
Rain. . . rain. . . rain. . . It's Christmas Day.

December 30
A buoy floated by. I baked an apple pie. I noticed sharp changes in the weather all day. I have a bad cold and am keeping the fire stoked until Ron returns from business in Louisville.

December 31
We had more rain. We had friends in and saw the old year out with the New Year's celebration in Times Square. We enjoyed ham and Swiss cheese with homemade mustard on onion-dill rolls.

Not everyone can live in a small town in the northwestern United States. Not everyone can observe wildlife in abundance, hear waves lapping against the shore of their property, and enjoy the changes of seasons throughout the year.

But everyone can enjoy the uniqueness of their particular bailiwick and exploit a region's charm. It might not be at the end of a ferry ride, but there will always be the blessings of family, work, recreation, and adventure.

Everyone needs places to play in
Where nature may heal and cheer and give strength.
—John Muir

Appendix

Berlinerkranser (butter rings)

3 hard-boiled egg yolks
4 raw egg yolks
1 cup, plus 2 tablespoons of sugar
1 pound of butter
5 to 5 ½ cups flour
1 egg white

Mash yolks of hard-boiled eggs. Add yolks of raw eggs, blending into a smooth paste. Add sugar, beating well.
Add flour and butter alternately, using your hands.
Roll pieces of dough to the thickness of a pencil, about three inches long. Shape each like a bow.
Whip egg white and brush on top of each cookie.
Bake at 350 degrees until light golden-brown. Makes seven dozen cookies.

We still use this recipe at each Christmas celebration. Store the cookies in a cool place. They also freeze well.

Other popular recipes include the following:

Squash in a Pumpkin

2 winter squash
2 apples
1 pumpkin
Cinnamon to taste
1/4 teaspoon ginger

Preheat oven to 400 degrees.
Bake apples and squash and a pumpkin (cut lid off pumpkin like jack o' lantern) for 1 hour.
Scrape seeds out of baked pumpkin shell
Stuff mashed squash and apple into the pumpkin shell.

Caramel Sauce for Pecan Rolls

½ cup brown sugar
¼ cup butter
1 tablespoon light corn syrup
Chopped pecans enough to cover bottom of pan

Combine ingredients and heat slowly, stirring often.
Put sauce on bottom of buttered pan and sprinkle with pecans.
Add favorite yeast cinnamon rolls.
Bake at 350 degrees for 20 minutes.

Lisa's Granola Chocolate-Chip Cookies

Original Nestle® Toll House® chocolate-chip cookie recipe on the package of chocolate chips, with the following changes:
Add a quarter cup less flour than Toll House recipe
Add only 1 cup chocolate chips

After you mix the ingredients for the Toll House cookies, proceed as follows:

EXTRA INGREDIENTS:

Add 1 cup of oats
Add 1 cup of unsweetened coconut.
Add 1 cup of chopped walnuts.
Add 1 cup of Quaker Natural Granola oats, honey, and raisins.
Mix in dry ingredients by hand.

The trick to the cookies is to use real butter (salted).

Ambrosia in Frozen Orange Shells

Woman's Day Cookbooks, volume 11, page 1,824

With sharp knife, cut oranges, zigzag, about one-third of the way down from top.
Scoop out pulp.
Freeze shells (or chill).
Combine pulp with chunks of pineapple.
Fill shells and sprinkle with grated coconut.
Garnish each with small leaf of mint

Grandma Pipho's Johnnycake

One cup of cornmeal
½ cup of sugar
4 teaspoons of baking powder
2 cups of flour
1 egg
1½ cups of milk
4 tablespoons of oil (Grandma used lard)

Mix in big bowl, and then bake at 350 degrees for 30 minutes.

Mom's Enchiladas

Use your favorite chili recipe, even your favorite can of chili.
1 cup of grated sharp-cheddar cheese
1 cup of chopped onions
A dozen corn tortillas

Sprinkle cheese and onions inside corn tortillas, and then roll them up.
In a small casserole pan, line the rolled corn tortillas tightly and cover with chili.
Bake at 350 degrees for 30 minutes.

Hershey's Old-Fashioned Cocoa Cake

2/3 cup butter 1 ¼ tsp baking soda
3/4 cup sugar 1 tsp salt
3 eggs 1/4 tsp baking powder
1/2 tsp vanilla 1 1/3 cups water
2 cups flour 2/3 cup cocoa

Beat butter, sugar, eggs and flour at high speed of mixer for four minutes. Combine dry ingredients; add alternately to creamed mixture. Blend just until combined. Pour into cocoa dusted cake pan. Bake at 350 degrees for 30 to 35 minutes.

Chocolate Cream Cheese Frosting

3 1 ounce squares of unsweetened Baker's Chocolate
4 tablespoons of cream or half and half
1 teaspoon of vanilla
6 ounces of softened cream cheese
1 tablespoon of soft butter
3 cups of confections sugar (I use sweetener to taste)

Place cream, vanilla, cheese and butter into blender for 15 seconds.

Add sugar and butter mixture slowly a little of each at a time until thoroughly blended. Frost cake.

Country Pumpkin Soup

1 cup chopped onion sautéed in 1/4 cup melted butter
29 oz and 16 oz can pumpkin
49 ½ oz can chicken broth
12 oz can evaporated milk
1/4 tsp salt
1/4 tsp marjoram
1/4 tsp thyme

Bring all ingredients to boil. Reduce heat. Simmer uncovered for 5 minutes.
Add a dash of hot pepper sauce.

Faith...sought the Lord since a girl

Adventure—decade living in High Sierras...machete in Ruth Runnels backyard

Professional—Real Estate lifestyle development/Writing

Achievements—Scholastic literary awards—created a lifestyle-special featured on HGTV

Background/Education—Azusa Pacific University/Fresno Pacific University

CPSIA information can be obtained at www.ICGtesting.com
Printed in the USA
LVOW041139161112

307628LV00001BD/1/P

9 781624 191824